From Conflict to Cooperation: Disarming for Development

By Robert Anderson Love Wins

http://RobertAndersonLoveWins.com

Table of Contents

Creating a strategy for safely moving governments around the world toward de-escalation and disarmament, while also protecting citizens' rights to bear arms and addressing the influences of corruption and profit motives associated with the war machine, is a complex but essential challenge. Here are several key components of a comprehensive strategy:

1. Diplomatic Engagement

Bilateral and Multilateral Dialogues

Facilitating constructive discussions between nations is essential for building trust and addressing pressing security concerns. These dialogues should encompass several key elements:

1. Trust-Building Initiatives: Engage in open and transparent communication to foster mutual understanding. Establishing regular forums for dialogue can help nations express their security needs and fears, paving the way for collaborative solutions.

2. Focus on Responsible Civilian Arms Ownership: Recognize the importance of responsible arms ownership among citizens as a component of national security. Discussions should emphasize best practices for regulation, safety, and education, ensuring that individual rights are respected while promoting public safety.

3. Addressing Corruption: Actively confront the influence of corruption in military affairs. These dialogues should include commitments to transparency in defense spending, procurement processes, and military contracts. Nations can share best

practices for combating corruption and hold each other accountable through joint initiatives.

4. Limiting Corporate Influence: Examine the role of corporate interests in shaping military policy and arms production. By fostering discussions on ethical procurement and reducing dependence on profit-driven motives, nations can work toward a defense strategy that prioritizes peace and security over corporate profits.

5. Collaborative Security Frameworks: Establish cooperative security frameworks that allow nations to jointly address threats without resorting to militarization. This could include intelligence sharing, joint training exercises, and cooperative responses to transnational challenges such as terrorism and organized crime.

By focusing on these elements within bilateral and multilateral dialogues, nations can create a foundation for lasting peace and security, ultimately leading to a more stable and harmonious global environment.

International Organizations

Leveraging established international organizations such as the United Nations, NATO, and regional alliances is crucial for promoting dialogue and collaborative efforts toward disarmament. Here's how these platforms can facilitate meaningful progress:

1. Promoting Dialogue: International organizations serve as neutral ground for nations to engage in dialogue, addressing security concerns and exploring disarmament initiatives. By organizing conferences, summits, and working groups, these organizations can facilitate discussions that bring together diverse perspectives and foster understanding.

2. Collaborative Disarmament Efforts: Organizations like the United Nations can spearhead global disarmament campaigns, encouraging member states to commit to disarmament treaties and agreements. This could include initiatives aimed at reducing stockpiles of nuclear, chemical, and conventional weapons, as well as promoting the peaceful resolution of conflicts.

3. Advocating for Transparency: These organizations can play a pivotal role in advocating for transparency in defense spending. By establishing guidelines and frameworks for reporting military expenditures, they can help nations maintain accountability and ensure that defense budgets are allocated responsibly and ethically.

4. Strengthening Accountability Mechanisms: International organizations can develop and implement mechanisms to hold nations accountable for their commitments to disarmament and transparency. This may involve regular reporting, peer reviews, and the establishment of independent monitoring bodies to assess compliance with disarmament agreements.

5. Facilitating Capacity Building: Organizations like NATO can provide technical assistance and resources to member states, helping them develop capacities for effective arms control and disarmament initiatives. This can include training programs,

workshops, and best practice sharing to enhance nations' abilities to manage their military inventories responsibly.

6. Encouraging Regional Cooperation: Regional organizations can tailor disarmament efforts to the unique security dynamics of their areas. By fostering cooperation among neighboring countries, these organizations can address local conflicts, promote mutual security interests, and advance disarmament goals in a context that is relevant to the member states involved.

7. Engaging Civil Society: By promoting the involvement of non-governmental organizations, think tanks, and civil society groups, international organizations can broaden the dialogue on disarmament. Engaging these stakeholders can enhance public awareness and support for disarmament initiatives, fostering a culture of peace and cooperation.

By effectively utilizing the platforms provided by international organizations, nations can work together to advance disarmament goals, promote transparency and accountability in defense spending, and ultimately contribute to a more peaceful and secure world.

2. Building Trust

Building trust among nations is essential for successful disarmament and conflict resolution. Confidence-building measures (CBMs) play a critical role in fostering a secure environment where countries can engage openly and collaboratively. Here are key components of effective trust-building initiatives:

1. Transparency Initiatives:

  - Sharing Military Data: Encourage nations to share information regarding military capabilities, troop movements, and defense budgets. This openness can help dispel misunderstandings and reduce suspicions, fostering a climate of trust.

  - Public Reporting: Implement mechanisms for public reporting on military expenditures and arms acquisitions. Transparency in defense spending can help ensure that resources are allocated for genuine security needs rather than for corrupt practices or excessive militarization.

2. Joint Military Exercises:

  - Collaborative Training: Organize joint military exercises that involve participating nations. These exercises can enhance cooperation, improve interoperability, and provide an opportunity for military personnel to engage with one another in a non-confrontational setting.

   - Scenario-Based Drills: Conduct scenario-based drills that focus on humanitarian assistance, disaster response, and peacekeeping operations. These activities can demonstrate a commitment to collaborative security efforts and mutual support in times of crisis.

3. Eradicating Corruption:

   - Anti-Corruption Frameworks: Develop and promote frameworks specifically aimed at eradicating corruption within defense sectors. This includes establishing clear policies, legal frameworks, and mechanisms to investigate and prosecute corrupt practices.

   - International Cooperation: Foster cooperation among nations to combat corruption in defense procurement and spending. This can involve sharing best practices, providing technical assistance, and engaging in joint efforts to enhance accountability.

4. Accountability Mechanisms:

   - Independent Oversight: Establish independent oversight bodies to monitor defense expenditures and ensure compliance with established guidelines. These bodies can conduct audits and assessments to verify that resources are being used appropriately and effectively.

   - Reporting Mechanisms: Implement reporting mechanisms that allow nations to periodically report on their defense spending and compliance with disarmament commitments. This can promote accountability and enhance trust among nations.

5. Engaging Civil Society:

   - Involvement of NGOs and Think Tanks: Encourage the participation of non-governmental organizations (NGOs), think tanks, and civil society in discussions about defense transparency and accountability. These groups can provide valuable insights, raise awareness, and advocate for reforms.

   - Public Awareness Campaigns: Launch public awareness campaigns that highlight the importance of transparency and accountability in defense spending. Engaging the public can create a culture of accountability and support for disarmament initiatives.

By implementing these confidence-building measures, nations can create a foundation of trust that is essential for successful dialogue and cooperation. This trust is vital not only for advancing disarmament efforts but also for fostering a more stable and peaceful international environment.

Third-Party Mediators

The involvement of third-party mediators can be instrumental in facilitating constructive dialogue between nations, especially when addressing sensitive issues like disarmament, individual rights, and corruption. Here are key aspects of utilizing neutral countries or organizations as mediators:

1. Neutral Facilitation:

  - Impartiality: Select mediators who are perceived as neutral and unbiased by all parties involved. This can help create a safe environment for open dialogue, allowing nations to express their concerns without fear of favoritism or manipulation.

  - Established Reputation: Engage with respected international organizations (e.g., the United Nations, the African Union) or countries known for their diplomatic neutrality (e.g., Switzerland, Norway) that have a track record of successful mediation.

2. Creating Respectful Dialogue:

   - Inclusive Participation: Ensure that all parties feel respected and heard during discussions. Mediators can facilitate each side's participation, ensuring that their voices are acknowledged in the negotiation process.

   - Cultural Sensitivity: Mediators should be well-versed in the cultural and political contexts of the parties involved. This understanding can help navigate sensitive topics and foster mutual respect.

3. Addressing Individual Rights:

   - Human Rights Advocacy: Mediators can advocate for the protection of individual rights during discussions, ensuring that the voices of citizens, including those advocating for responsible arms ownership, are taken into account.

   - Focus on Inclusivity: Promote the inclusion of civil society representatives in discussions, allowing for broader perspectives that encompass the needs and rights of the population.

4. Combating Corruption:

  - Transparency Initiatives: Mediators can help establish frameworks for transparency in defense spending and military agreements. This may include recommending independent audits and monitoring mechanisms to ensure compliance.

  - Best Practices Sharing: Facilitate the sharing of best practices among nations for combating corruption in defense sectors, drawing upon successful models from other countries or regions.

5. Conflict Resolution Frameworks:

  - Structured Processes: Mediators can provide structured frameworks for discussions, helping to identify key issues, establish agendas, and facilitate negotiations in an organized manner.

  - Ongoing Support: Offer continuous support throughout the negotiation process, including follow-up discussions and assistance in implementing agreements reached, ensuring that commitments are upheld.

6. Building Long-Term Relationships:

  - Trust Development: Mediators can play a vital role in building long-term relationships between nations, fostering trust and cooperation that extend beyond the immediate discussions.

  - Capacity Building: Encourage capacity-building initiatives that enhance the skills of negotiators and diplomats from all parties, promoting sustainable dialogue practices.

By utilizing third-party mediators effectively, nations can create a conducive environment for dialogue that prioritizes respect, inclusivity, and accountability. This approach is essential for addressing complex issues related to disarmament, individual rights, and corruption, ultimately contributing to a more peaceful and stable international landscape.

3. Public Awareness and Education

Raising public awareness and educating communities about disarmament, peaceful conflict resolution, and responsible gun ownership is vital for fostering a culture of peace and understanding. Here are key elements of effective global awareness campaigns:

1. Comprehensive Campaign Strategies:

- Multimedia Outreach: Utilize various media platforms—including social media, television, radio, and print—to disseminate information about the benefits of disarmament and peaceful conflict resolution. Engaging content, such as documentaries, infographics, and podcasts, can help reach diverse audiences.

- Targeted Messaging: Tailor messages to different demographics and cultural contexts to ensure that the information resonates with specific communities. This can enhance engagement and foster a deeper understanding of the issues at hand.

2. Educational Programs:

   - School Curricula: Integrate topics related to disarmament, conflict resolution, and responsible gun ownership into educational curricula at all levels. This can empower young people to understand the importance of peace and the impact of militarization on society.

   - Workshops and Seminars: Organize workshops, seminars, and community forums that facilitate discussions on the implications of militarization, the importance of disarmament, and the responsibilities of gun ownership. These events can encourage active participation and critical thinking.

3. Highlighting the Dangers of Militarization:

   - Research and Reporting: Publish reports and studies that illustrate the negative consequences of militarization driven by profit motives, including social, economic, and environmental impacts. Sharing data and real-life case studies can help raise awareness about the urgency of disarmament.

   - Storytelling: Use personal narratives and testimonials from individuals affected by militarization and conflict to humanize the issue and foster empathy. Stories can be powerful tools for inspiring change and encouraging public support for disarmament initiatives.

4. Promoting Responsible Gun Ownership:

   - Safety Campaigns: Launch campaigns that emphasize the importance of responsible gun ownership, including safe storage practices, training, and education. Highlighting the role of gun owners in promoting safety can help mitigate risks associated with firearm misuse.

   - Community Engagement: Collaborate with local organizations, law enforcement, and community leaders to promote responsible gun ownership and safety training programs. Engaging communities in discussions around gun rights and responsibilities can foster a culture of accountability.

5. Encouraging Dialogue and Participation:

   - Public Forums and Debates: Host public forums and debates that encourage open discussions about disarmament, gun ownership, and militarization. Creating a safe space for dialogue can empower citizens to voice their opinions and contribute to the conversation.

   - Engaging Influencers: Partner with influential figures, celebrities, and community leaders who can champion disarmament initiatives and responsible gun ownership. Their platforms can amplify the message and reach wider audiences.

6. Global Collaboration:

- Partnerships with NGOs: Collaborate with non-governmental organizations, think tanks, and advocacy groups focused on peacebuilding and disarmament. These partnerships can enhance the effectiveness of campaigns by pooling resources and expertise.

- International Events: Participate in international events and observances focused on peace, disarmament, and gun safety. These occasions can serve as catalysts for broader discussions and mobilize global support for the cause.

By implementing comprehensive public awareness campaigns, nations and organizations can educate communities about the critical importance of disarmament, peaceful conflict resolution, and responsible gun ownership. This collective effort can help foster a more informed and engaged public, ultimately contributing to a culture of peace and reducing the influence of militarization and profit motives in society.

Engaging influential leaders, celebrities, and activists can significantly amplify the message of disarmament initiatives, responsible arms rights, and the need to combat corruption in military and defense industries. Here are key strategies for effectively collaborating with influencers:

1. Identifying the Right Influencers:

 - Relevance and Alignment: Select influencers whose values and missions align with the goals of disarmament and responsible arms rights. This includes individuals from diverse fields such as politics, entertainment, sports, and social activism.

 - Reach and Impact: Consider influencers who have a substantial following and the ability to reach various demographics. Their platforms can help disseminate messages to a broader audience.

2. Building Collaborative Partnerships:

 - Joint Campaigns: Develop campaigns in collaboration with influencers that promote disarmament initiatives and responsible arms ownership. This can include joint public service announcements, social media campaigns, and community events.

- Co-Creation of Content: Work with influencers to create engaging content, such as videos, blogs, and podcasts, that highlight the importance of disarmament and the risks associated with militarization and corruption.

3. Leveraging Social Media:

- Amplifying Messages: Encourage influencers to use their social media platforms to share information, personal stories, and calls to action related to disarmament and responsible arms rights. Hashtags, challenges, and interactive content can further engage their followers.

- Live Discussions and Q&A: Host live discussions or Q&A sessions on social media where influencers can engage with their audiences about disarmament issues, answer questions, and share insights. This interactive approach fosters deeper engagement.

4. Highlighting Personal Stories:

- Testimonials: Encourage influencers to share their personal stories or experiences related to disarmament, gun ownership, or the impact of corruption in the defense industry. Authentic narratives can resonate with audiences and inspire action.

- Advocacy Through Experience: Leverage the unique backgrounds and experiences of influencers to highlight the importance of responsible arms rights and the need for transparency in military spending.

5. Engaging in Advocacy and Events:

- Public Appearances: Collaborate with influencers to participate in events, rallies, and conferences focused on disarmament and arms rights. Their presence can draw attention and encourage greater public participation.

- Advocacy Days: Organize advocacy days where influencers can meet with policymakers and stakeholders to discuss the importance of disarmament, responsible arms ownership, and anti-corruption measures.

6. Fostering Long-Term Relationships:

- Ongoing Collaboration: Establish long-term partnerships with influencers, allowing for sustained engagement and advocacy over time. This can help maintain momentum and keep the issues of disarmament and responsible arms rights in the public eye.

- Recognition and Support: Acknowledge and support the work of influencers in this space, celebrating their contributions and promoting their efforts to raise awareness about disarmament and accountability.

7. Measuring Impact:

  - Tracking Engagement: Monitor the reach and engagement of influencer campaigns to assess their effectiveness. Metrics such as social media shares, comments, and participation in events can provide insights into the campaign's impact.

  - Feedback and Adaptation: Solicit feedback from influencers and their audiences to refine strategies and improve future collaborations.

By engaging influential figures in the advocacy for disarmament initiatives, responsible arms rights, and the fight against corruption in military and defense industries, organizations can leverage their reach and credibility to create a more significant impact. This collaborative approach can help raise awareness, inspire action, and foster a culture of peace and accountability within society.

4. Economic Incentives

Sanctions and Rewards

Utilizing a strategy of sanctions and rewards can effectively promote disarmament while respecting civilian rights and addressing issues of corruption and profit motives in military operations. Here are key components of this approach:

1. Economic Incentives for Disarmament:

   - Conditional Lifting of Sanctions: Implement a framework where sanctions imposed on countries for military aggression or nuclear proliferation can be lifted in exchange for tangible commitments to disarmament. This approach encourages nations to take concrete steps toward reducing armaments while providing an economic incentive for compliance.

   - Financial Aid and Support: Offer financial assistance or development aid to countries that commit to disarmament initiatives. This can help nations redirect resources from military spending to social programs, education, and infrastructure development.

2. Monitoring Compliance:

- Implementation of Verification Mechanisms: Establish robust verification systems to ensure compliance with disarmament commitments. Independent monitoring bodies can assess whether nations are following through on their promises, providing transparency and accountability.

- Regular Reporting: Require nations to submit periodic reports detailing their progress in disarmament efforts. This can help maintain pressure on governments to adhere to their commitments while allowing the international community to assess the effectiveness of the initiatives.

3. Addressing Corruption:

- Anti-Corruption Initiatives: Incorporate anti-corruption measures into the sanctions and rewards framework. Nations receiving financial aid or incentives should demonstrate efforts to combat corruption within their defense sectors, ensuring that funds are used responsibly.

- Transparency in Defense Spending: Encourage recipient nations to adopt transparent practices in defense procurement and budgeting. This can help build trust and ensure that resources are allocated toward peacebuilding rather than military expansion.

4. Promoting Responsible Arms Trade:

- Conditional Arms Sales: Implement policies that condition arms sales to countries based on their commitment to disarmament and responsible arms management. Nations that demonstrate progress in reducing military stockpiles could receive favorable trade terms or support for defense modernization that prioritizes safety and accountability.

- Collaboration with International Bodies: Work with organizations such as the United Nations to establish global norms and guidelines for arms trade that prioritize disarmament and responsible ownership, discouraging illicit arms trading and promoting accountability.

5. Engaging Civil Society:

- Inclusion of Civil Society Organizations: Involve civil society organizations in the design and implementation of sanctions and rewards frameworks. Their insights can help ensure that the measures are effective and take into account the perspectives of affected populations.

- Public Awareness Campaigns: Launch campaigns to inform the public about the rationale behind sanctions and rewards, emphasizing the importance of disarmament and responsible arms ownership. Engaging citizens can create a supportive environment for these initiatives.

6. Long-Term Sustainability:

  - Focus on Sustainable Development: Align rewards with sustainable development goals to address the root causes of conflict and militarization. Investments in education, healthcare, and economic development can contribute to long-term stability and reduce the reliance on military solutions.

  - Building Partnerships: Foster partnerships between nations, NGOs, and international organizations to create a collaborative approach to disarmament. This can enhance the effectiveness of sanctions and rewards by pooling resources and expertise.

By strategically using sanctions and rewards, the international community can promote disarmament while safeguarding civilian rights and addressing corruption and profit motives in military operations. This balanced approach can help create a more secure and peaceful world, where nations are incentivized to prioritize disarmament and responsible governance.

Investing in peacebuilding is essential for creating sustainable stability and reducing reliance on military expenditure. By prioritizing social programs, education, and infrastructure, governments and organizations can foster environments where peace thrives and responsible arms ownership is upheld. Here are key components of this investment strategy:

1. Social Programs:

 - Community Development Initiatives: Fund programs that strengthen community cohesion, such as conflict resolution workshops, community dialogues, and intercultural exchange initiatives. These efforts can help build relationships and trust among diverse groups, reducing the likelihood of conflict.

 - Mental Health and Counseling Services: Provide access to mental health resources and counseling services to address trauma and promote emotional well-being, particularly in communities affected by violence. Supporting mental health can contribute to overall community stability and resilience.

2. Education:

 - Quality Education Access: Invest in education systems that provide quality education to all children, emphasizing critical thinking, conflict resolution, and civic education. Educated citizens are better equipped to engage in peaceful dialogue and contribute to society constructively.

   - Vocational Training Programs: Establish vocational training and skills development programs that offer job opportunities to youth and marginalized groups. Economic stability can reduce the appeal of joining armed groups or engaging in violence.

3. Infrastructure Development:

   - Building Essential Services: Invest in infrastructure projects that provide essential services, such as clean water, healthcare, and transportation. Improved infrastructure can enhance living conditions and promote economic growth, reducing the need for military expenditure.

   - Safe Spaces for Community Engagement: Create safe public spaces where communities can gather, share ideas, and engage in dialogue. These spaces can foster a sense of belonging and community ownership, which is vital for maintaining peace.

4. Promoting Responsible Arms Ownership:

   - Educational Campaigns on Firearm Safety: Develop campaigns that educate citizens about responsible arms ownership, including safe storage practices and the importance of training. This can empower individuals to own firearms safely and responsibly, aligning with their rights while promoting public safety.

  - Support for Regulatory Frameworks: Encourage governments to establish and enforce regulations that ensure responsible arms ownership while balancing individual rights and community safety. This includes background checks, licensing, and training requirements.

5. Encouraging Community Involvement:

  - Local Participation in Decision-Making: Foster community involvement in peacebuilding initiatives and decision-making processes. Engaging local populations can lead to more effective and culturally sensitive programs that address specific needs and concerns.

  - Volunteering and Community Service Programs: Promote volunteerism and community service programs that encourage citizens to contribute to peacebuilding efforts. These initiatives can strengthen community bonds and empower individuals to take an active role in promoting peace.

6. Long-Term Sustainability:

  - Aligning Investments with Sustainable Development Goals (SDGs): Ensure that investments in peacebuilding align with the United Nations Sustainable Development Goals. Addressing issues such as poverty, inequality, and education can create a more stable foundation for lasting peace.

- Monitoring and Evaluation: Establish mechanisms to monitor and evaluate the impact of peacebuilding investments. Assessing the effectiveness of programs can help refine approaches and ensure that resources are used efficiently.

7. International Collaboration:

- Partnerships with NGOs and International Organizations: Collaborate with non-governmental organizations and international bodies to leverage resources and expertise in peacebuilding efforts. These partnerships can enhance the effectiveness of initiatives and promote best practices globally.

- Funding and Support from Global Institutions: Seek funding and support from international financial institutions and donor countries to invest in peacebuilding initiatives. Sustainable funding can ensure the longevity and impact of these programs.

By investing in peacebuilding through social programs, education, and infrastructure, societies can create environments that promote stability, reduce the need for military expenditure, and support responsible arms ownership. This comprehensive approach not only addresses the immediate needs of communities but also lays the groundwork for a more peaceful and secure future.

5. Arms Control Agreements

Advocating for and negotiating arms control treaties is a crucial step toward limiting the production and proliferation of weapons, ensuring global security, and addressing the influence of corporate interests in defense manufacturing. Here are key components of this approach:

1. Establishing Clear Objectives:

- Define Treaty Goals: Clearly outline the objectives of arms control treaties, such as limiting specific types of weapons, reducing stockpiles, and preventing the proliferation of advanced military technologies. Setting measurable targets can facilitate accountability and compliance.

- Focus on Humanitarian Impact: Emphasize the humanitarian consequences of arms proliferation, including the impact on civilian populations and the environment. Treaties should consider the broader implications of weapons production and usage on global peace and security.

2. Inclusive Negotiation Processes:

- Engage Diverse Stakeholders: Involve a wide range of stakeholders in the negotiation process, including government representatives, civil society organizations, and experts in disarmament and arms control. This inclusive approach can lead to more comprehensive and effective treaties.

- Address Corporate Interests: Recognize and address the influence of corporate interests in defense manufacturing during negotiations. Establish guidelines that limit lobbying and ensure that treaties prioritize public safety and global security over corporate profits.

3. Robust Verification Mechanisms:

- Implement Verification Protocols: Establish clear verification mechanisms to ensure compliance with treaty provisions. This can include regular inspections, audits, and reporting requirements to monitor weapon production and stockpiles.

- Utilize Technology: Leverage technology, such as satellite monitoring and data-sharing platforms, to enhance transparency and verification efforts. Technological advancements can provide real-time data on military activities and compliance.

4. International Cooperation:

- Collaborate with International Organizations: Work with organizations such as the United Nations, the Organization for

Security and Co-operation in Europe (OSCE), and regional bodies to facilitate treaty negotiations and implementation. These organizations can provide platforms for dialogue and resources for monitoring compliance.

   - Promote Regional Treaties: Encourage the development of regional arms control treaties that address specific security challenges and dynamics. Regional agreements can complement global efforts and foster cooperation among neighboring nations.

5. Public Awareness and Advocacy:

   - Raise Public Awareness: Launch campaigns to educate the public about the importance of arms control treaties and their implications for global security. Engaging citizens can create public support for disarmament efforts and hold governments accountable for treaty commitments.

   - Involve Influential Advocates: Collaborate with influential figures, including activists, academics, and former military leaders, to advocate for arms control treaties. Their voices can amplify the message and encourage broader engagement.

6. Addressing Non-State Actors:

   - Include Provisions for Non-State Actors: Recognize the role of non-state actors in arms proliferation and include provisions in treaties that address the challenges posed by illicit arms trafficking and the activities of armed groups.

- Strengthen Border Control Measures: Advocate for enhanced border control and law enforcement cooperation to prevent the flow of illegal people and arms to combat the activities of non-state actors.

7. Long-Term Commitment and Review:

- Establish Review Mechanisms: Create frameworks for periodic reviews of treaty effectiveness and compliance. Regular assessments can help identify challenges and opportunities for improvement, ensuring that treaties remain relevant and effective.

- Foster Long-Term Engagement: Encourage ongoing dialogue and collaboration among signatory states to address emerging security threats and adapt arms control measures as necessary.

By advocating for and negotiating arms control treaties that limit the production and proliferation of weapons, while considering the impact of corporate interests in defense manufacturing, nations can work toward a more secure and peaceful world. This comprehensive approach not only addresses immediate security concerns but also lays the groundwork for a culture of responsibility and accountability in global arms management.

Verification Mechanisms

Establishing robust verification processes is essential for ensuring compliance with disarmament agreements. These mechanisms must be designed to promote transparency, build trust among nations, and respect the rights of citizens while effectively combating corruption in the defense sector. Here are key components of effective verification mechanisms:

1. Comprehensive Frameworks:

  - Clear Guidelines: Develop detailed guidelines outlining the verification process, including the specific obligations of each party under the disarmament agreement. These guidelines should clarify the scope, methods, and frequency of inspections and reporting requirements.

  - Inclusive Participation: Involve a diverse range of stakeholders in the development of verification frameworks, including government representatives, independent experts, civil society organizations, and affected communities. This inclusivity can enhance the legitimacy and effectiveness of the verification process.

2. Inspection Protocols:

- Regular Inspections: Establish protocols for regular inspections of military facilities, stockpiles, and production sites to ensure compliance with disarmament commitments. Inspections should be conducted by independent third-party experts to guarantee impartiality.

- Surprise Inspections: Incorporate provisions for unannounced inspections to deter non-compliance and ensure that nations adhere to their commitments. Surprise inspections can enhance accountability and transparency.

3. Monitoring Technologies:

- Utilization of Technology: Leverage advanced monitoring technologies, such as satellite imagery, remote sensing, and data analytics, to track military activities and assess compliance with disarmament agreements. Technology can provide real-time data and enhance the effectiveness of verification efforts.

- Data Sharing Platforms: Create secure data-sharing platforms that allow nations to share information related to disarmament and compliance. This transparency can build trust among parties and facilitate collaborative monitoring efforts.

4. Reporting Requirements:

- Regular Reporting: Mandate regular reporting from signatory nations on their disarmament progress, including details on weapon stockpiles, production activities, and compliance with treaty obligations. Reports should be made publicly accessible to enhance transparency.

- Independent Audits: Incorporate independent audits of defense spending and arms management practices as part of the reporting process. Audits can help identify instances of corruption and ensure that resources are used appropriately.

5. Citizen Engagement:

- Public Awareness and Education: Educate citizens about the disarmament agreements and verification processes to foster public support and engagement. Informed citizens can hold their governments accountable and advocate for transparency in defense practices.

- Involvement of Civil Society: Encourage the participation of civil society organizations in the verification process. These organizations can act as watchdogs, monitoring compliance and advocating for accountability and transparency.

6. Addressing Corruption:

- Anti-Corruption Measures: Integrate anti-corruption provisions into verification processes, including mechanisms for reporting and investigating allegations of corruption within the defense sector. Establishing clear penalties for violations can deter corrupt practices.

 - Transparency in Defense Procurement: Promote transparency in defense procurement processes, ensuring that contracts and spending are publicly disclosed and subject to independent oversight. This transparency can help mitigate the influence of corruption in arms management.

7. Long-Term Adaptability:

 - Periodic Review and Assessment: Establish mechanisms for periodic review and assessment of verification processes to identify areas for improvement and adapt to changing security environments. Regular evaluations can ensure that verification frameworks remain effective and relevant.

 - Flexibility in Implementation: Allow for flexibility in the implementation of verification mechanisms to accommodate the unique circumstances of different nations while maintaining core principles of transparency and accountability.

By establishing robust verification mechanisms that include inspections, monitoring, and reporting processes, nations can ensure compliance with disarmament agreements while respecting citizens' rights and combating corruption in the defense sector. These mechanisms are vital for building trust, enhancing accountability, and promoting a culture of peace and security in the international community.

6. Crisis Management Frameworks

Early Warning Systems

Developing effective early warning systems is essential for detecting rising tensions between nations and facilitating timely intervention to prevent conflicts from escalating. These systems must focus on safeguarding civilian rights and addressing the influence of military interests in decision-making. Here are key components to consider when establishing early warning systems:

1. Comprehensive Data Collection:

   - Multi-Sourced Intelligence: Utilize a wide range of data sources, including diplomatic communications, media reports, social media analysis, economic indicators, and military movements. Comprehensive data collection can provide a holistic view of potential conflicts.

   - Community-Level Input: Incorporate input from local communities, civil society organizations, and grassroots movements to capture on-the-ground sentiments and tensions. Engaging local voices can help identify emerging issues that may not be reflected in official sources.

2. Advanced Analytical Tools:

- Predictive Analytics: Employ advanced analytical tools and algorithms to analyze collected data and identify patterns that may indicate rising tensions. Predictive analytics can help assess the likelihood of conflict escalation and inform timely interventions.

- Risk Assessment Frameworks: Develop frameworks to assess the risk of conflict based on various factors, including historical grievances, resource competition, and socio-political dynamics. These frameworks can aid in prioritizing areas for intervention and support.

3. Continuous Monitoring:

- Real-Time Monitoring: Establish real-time monitoring systems that continuously track relevant indicators of tension, such as military deployments, political rhetoric, economic sanctions, and humanitarian crises. Continuous monitoring allows for prompt identification of escalating situations.

- Regional and Global Networks: Create networks for information sharing among nations, international organizations, and regional bodies. Collaborative monitoring can enhance situational awareness and facilitate coordinated responses.

4. Timely Reporting and Communication:

- Early Warning Alerts: Develop mechanisms for issuing early warning alerts to relevant stakeholders, including governments, international organizations, and civil society. Alerts should be timely, clear, and actionable, providing specific recommendations for intervention.

- Transparent Communication: Ensure transparency in the reporting process to build trust among stakeholders. Open communication about the nature of the threats and the rationale for interventions can help reduce misunderstandings and foster cooperation.

5. Focus on Civilian Rights:

- Human Rights Considerations: Ensure that early warning systems incorporate assessments of potential human rights violations and the impact on civilian populations. Monitoring for indicators of repression or violence against civilians is critical in conflict prevention.

- Engaging Civil Society: Involve civil society organizations in the early warning process to ensure that the rights and perspectives of affected communities are considered. Their involvement can enhance the effectiveness of interventions.

6. Addressing the Influence of Military Interests:

- Assessing Military Dynamics: Analyze the role of military interests and defense industries in escalating tensions. Understanding how the war machine influences political decisions can provide insights into the root causes of conflict.

- Promoting Non-Military Solutions: Encourage discussions around non-military solutions to emerging tensions, emphasizing diplomacy, dialogue, and negotiation. Early warning systems should advocate for peaceful interventions rather than militarized responses.

7. Institutional Support and Capacity Building:

- Training and Capacity Development: Provide training for diplomats, peacekeepers, and civil society organizations on the use of early warning systems. Building local capacity to interpret and act on early warning data can strengthen conflict prevention efforts.

- Collaboration with International Organizations: Partner with international organizations, such as the United Nations and regional bodies, to enhance the effectiveness of early warning systems. Collaborative efforts can leverage resources, expertise, and networks for conflict prevention.

8. Evaluation and Adaptation:

- Regular Review of Effectiveness: Establish mechanisms for the periodic evaluation of early warning systems to assess their effectiveness and adapt to changing geopolitical landscapes. Continuous improvement can enhance the systems' ability to prevent conflicts.

- Feedback Loops: Create feedback loops to incorporate lessons learned and best practices from past interventions. An adaptive approach can enhance the responsiveness of early warning systems to emerging challenges.

By developing comprehensive early warning systems that prioritize civilian rights and address the influence of military interests, nations can proactively detect rising tensions and implement timely interventions to prevent conflicts from escalating. This approach fosters a culture of peace and cooperation, ultimately contributing to greater global stability.

Establishing effective crisis response mechanisms is essential for addressing conflicts swiftly and preventing escalation. These protocols should include diplomatic interventions, conflict resolution strategies, and considerations of profit motives that may exacerbate violence. Here are key components to consider when creating crisis response mechanisms:

1. Protocol Development:

   - Standard Operating Procedures (SOPs): Develop clear and comprehensive SOPs for various types of crises, including armed conflicts, humanitarian disasters, and political upheavals. These protocols should outline specific steps for intervention, roles and responsibilities, and communication strategies.

   - Multi-Agency Coordination: Ensure that crisis response protocols facilitate coordination among relevant agencies, including government bodies, international organizations, NGOs, and local communities. A collaborative approach can enhance the effectiveness of responses.

2. Rapid Response Teams:

- Formation of Response Units: Establish dedicated rapid response teams composed of diplomats, conflict resolution experts, humanitarian workers, and relevant stakeholders. These teams should be trained and prepared to deploy quickly to areas experiencing crises.

- Enhanced Trained Personnel: Invest in training personnel in conflict resolution, negotiation, mediation, and cultural sensitivity. Skilled responders can engage effectively with affected communities and navigate complex situations.

3. Diplomatic Interventions:

- Preemptive Diplomacy: Encourage the use of preemptive diplomacy to address emerging tensions before they escalate into full-blown crises. This may involve engaging in dialogue with key stakeholders, offering mediation services, and facilitating negotiations.

- Track II Diplomacy: Promote unofficial dialogue channels, known as Track II diplomacy, involving non-governmental actors, influential civil society members, and community leaders. These informal conversations can complement official negotiations and help build trust.

4. Conflict Resolution Strategies:

- Mediation and Facilitation: Implement structured mediation processes that bring conflicting parties together to identify common ground and work toward peaceful resolutions. Skilled mediators can help parties articulate their concerns and find mutually acceptable solutions.

- Inclusive Dialogue Processes: Ensure that crisis response strategies include diverse perspectives, particularly from marginalized and affected communities. Inclusive dialogue fosters ownership of solutions and enhances the legitimacy of interventions.

5. Addressing Profit Motives:

- Analysis of Economic Drivers: Conduct analyses to identify the profit motives that may contribute to escalating violence, such as arms trade, resource exploitation, and military contracts. Understanding these dynamics can inform more effective responses.

- Promoting Ethical Practices: Advocate for ethical practices in the defense industry and arms trade, emphasizing corporate responsibility. Encourage businesses to adopt guidelines that prioritize peace and stability over profit.

6. Humanitarian Assistance:

- Integrated Humanitarian Response: Incorporate humanitarian assistance into crisis response protocols, ensuring that immediate needs for food, shelter, healthcare, and protection are addressed alongside conflict resolution efforts.

- Support for Local Capacity: Empower local organizations and communities to respond to crises by providing resources, training, and support. Local actors often have valuable insights and connections that can enhance response efforts.

7. Monitoring and Evaluation:

- Real-Time Monitoring: Establish systems for real-time monitoring of crises to assess the effectiveness of interventions and adapt strategies as needed. Continuous assessment can help responders remain agile and responsive to changing circumstances.

- Post-Crisis Evaluation: Conduct evaluations after crises have been addressed to identify lessons learned, successes, and areas for improvement. This feedback can inform future crisis response protocols and enhance preparedness.

8. Long-Term Solutions:

- Addressing Root Causes: Develop strategies that address the underlying causes of conflict, including social, economic, and political grievances. Long-term solutions can help prevent future crises and promote sustainable peace.

   - Building Resilience: Invest in community resilience initiatives that empower populations to manage and mitigate crises effectively. Resilient communities can better withstand shocks and contribute to stability.

By creating comprehensive crisis response mechanisms that include diplomatic interventions, conflict resolution strategies, and an understanding of profit motives in escalating violence, nations can respond more effectively to crises and work toward sustainable peace. This proactive approach not only addresses immediate conflicts but also lays the foundation for long-term stability and cooperation.

7. Cultural Exchange and Cooperation

Promote Cultural Exchanges

Encouraging cultural exchanges can play a significant role in fostering understanding and cooperation between nations, creating a foundation for dialogue on critical issues such as responsible arms ownership and the influence of the military-industrial complex. Here are key components and strategies for promoting effective cultural exchange programs:

1. Diverse Exchange Programs:

   - Student and Academic Exchanges: Facilitate programs that allow students and scholars to study abroad, engage in research, and participate in academic discussions. These exchanges can promote cross-cultural understanding and collaborative learning on issues related to arms control and conflict resolution.

   - Art and Cultural Festivals: Organize festivals that celebrate diverse cultures, showcasing art, music, and performances from different nations. Such events can foster appreciation for cultural diversity while providing a platform for discussions on shared global challenges.

2. Workshops and Dialogue Initiatives:

- Responsible Arms Ownership Workshops: Conduct workshops that bring together participants from various countries to discuss the principles of responsible arms ownership, highlighting best practices and lessons learned. These discussions can promote safe and ethical firearms management across cultures.

- Military-Industrial Complex Forums: Organize forums that facilitate open discussions about the influence of the military-industrial complex on policy and society. Engaging diverse voices can help raise awareness of this issue and encourage collaborative approaches to mitigate its impact.

3. Collaborative Research Projects:

- Joint Research Initiatives: Encourage collaborative research projects that involve scholars and practitioners from different countries. These projects can focus on issues such as disarmament, conflict resolution, and the socio-economic impacts of militarization, fostering a shared understanding of challenges and solutions.

- Policy Exchange Programs: Create opportunities for policymakers to engage in dialogue and share experiences related to arms control, military spending, and community safety. Such exchanges can inform policy development and promote best practices.

4. Community-Based Initiatives:

  - Local Partnerships: Facilitate partnerships between organizations in different countries to implement community-based programs that promote peace and understanding. These initiatives can address local issues related to arms ownership and militarization while fostering cross-cultural connections.

  - Youth Engagement Programs: Develop programs specifically targeting youth to engage them in discussions about peace, responsible arms ownership, and the impacts of militarization. Empowering young people can cultivate a new generation of advocates for peace and responsibility.

5. Utilizing Digital Platforms:

  - Virtual Exchange Programs: Leverage digital technology to create virtual exchange programs that connect individuals and groups from different countries. Online discussions, webinars, and collaborative projects can foster understanding without the barriers of physical distance.

  - Social Media Campaigns: Utilize social media platforms to promote cultural exchanges and discussions on arms ownership and military influences. Engaging narratives, videos, and infographics can help raise awareness and encourage dialogue across borders.

6. Promoting Ethical Considerations:

   - Cultural Sensitivity Training: Incorporate cultural sensitivity training into exchange programs to ensure participants understand and respect the diverse perspectives and values of other cultures. This training can enhance the effectiveness of discussions and collaborations.

   - Highlighting Ethical Arms Trade: Foster discussions that emphasize the importance of ethical considerations in arms trade and ownership. Engaging diverse voices can highlight the need for accountability and responsible practices.

7. Evaluation and Impact Assessment:

   - Measuring Program Effectiveness: Implement mechanisms to evaluate the impact of cultural exchange programs on fostering understanding and cooperation. Collecting feedback and assessing outcomes can help refine and improve future initiatives.

   - Sharing Success Stories: Document and share success stories from cultural exchange programs that have led to positive outcomes in responsible arms ownership and combatting militarization. Highlighting these examples can inspire further engagement and investment in similar initiatives.

By promoting cultural exchanges that emphasize understanding, cooperation, and dialogue on responsible arms ownership and the military-industrial complex, nations can foster a more peaceful and collaborative international community. These efforts can contribute to breaking down barriers, building trust, and encouraging collective action toward common goals.

Engaging local communities is essential for fostering dialogue and understanding among diverse cultural and ethnic groups. Supporting grassroots initiatives can help address pressing issues such as corruption and militarization while promoting personal and collective security. Here are key components and strategies for effective community engagement:

1. Community Dialogue Programs:

 - Facilitated Discussions: Organize facilitated dialogue sessions that bring together individuals from different cultural and ethnic backgrounds to discuss their experiences, concerns, and aspirations. Trained facilitators can help create a safe and respectful environment for open conversations.

 - Thematic Workshops: Host workshops focused on specific topics, such as the implications of militarization, the impact of corruption, and the importance of community safety. These workshops can provide a platform for sharing knowledge and developing collaborative solutions.

2. Collaborative Community Projects:

 - Joint Initiatives: Encourage community members from diverse backgrounds to collaborate on projects that address shared challenges. Examples include community clean-up efforts, educational programs, or local art initiatives that promote peace and understanding.

  - Problem-Solving Groups: Establish community problem-solving groups that focus on identifying and addressing local issues related to corruption and militarization. Involving residents in the decision-making process can empower them and foster a sense of ownership over solutions.

3. Educational Outreach:

  - Awareness Campaigns: Develop awareness campaigns that educate community members about the effects of corruption and militarization on their lives and security. Utilize various media channels, including social media, local newspapers, and community bulletin boards, to disseminate information.

  - Youth Engagement Programs: Create programs specifically for youth that encourage critical thinking about issues related to corruption and militarization. Workshops, debates, and art projects can engage young people and empower them to advocate for positive change.

4. Cultural Exchange and Appreciation:

  - Cultural Events: Organize cultural events that celebrate the diversity of the community, such as festivals, art exhibitions, and performances. These events can foster appreciation for different cultures and promote dialogue among community members.

- Storytelling Initiatives: Encourage individuals from various backgrounds to share their stories and experiences related to security, corruption, and militarization. Storytelling can humanize these issues and build empathy among community members.

5. Building Trust and Relationships:

- Community Trust-Building Initiatives: Implement trust-building activities that encourage interaction and collaboration among different groups within the community. Trust-building exercises can help break down barriers and foster mutual respect.

- Engaging Local Leaders: Work with local leaders, including religious figures, educators, and respected community members, to facilitate discussions and promote initiatives. Their involvement can lend credibility and encourage broader participation.

6. Addressing Corruption and Security:

- Transparency Initiatives: Support initiatives that promote transparency in local governance and community decision-making. Engaging citizens in discussions about accountability can empower them to demand integrity from their leaders.

- Security Assessments: Conduct community assessments to identify local perceptions of security and the impact of corruption and militarization. Gathering input from residents can inform targeted interventions that address their specific concerns.

7. Feedback and Adaptation:

- Continuous Feedback Loop: Establish mechanisms for ongoing feedback from community members regarding the effectiveness of engagement initiatives. Regularly soliciting input can help refine strategies and ensure that programs remain responsive to community needs.

- Sharing Outcomes: Document and share the outcomes of community engagement initiatives, highlighting successes and lessons learned. Sharing these narratives can inspire other communities to adopt similar approaches.

8. Long-Term Commitment:

- Sustainable Community Partnerships: Foster long-term partnerships between local organizations, government agencies, and community members to ensure the sustainability of engagement initiatives. Collaborative efforts can enhance capacity building and create lasting impact.

- Ongoing Training and Support: Provide ongoing training and resources for community leaders and facilitators to enhance their skills in conflict resolution, dialogue facilitation, and community organizing.

By engaging local communities in initiatives that promote dialogue and understanding, especially regarding the implications of corruption and militarization, societies can build stronger, more resilient communities. These efforts empower individuals to take an active role in shaping their collective security and foster a culture of peace, cooperation, and accountability.

8. Long-Term Vision

Global Disarmament Goals

Establishing a long-term vision for global disarmament requires a comprehensive approach that includes specific, achievable goals, timelines, and accountability measures for participating nations. This vision must also prioritize the rights of responsible civilian arms owners and actively combat corruption within the defense sector. Here are key components to consider when formulating global disarmament goals:

1. Setting Clear Objectives:

- Specific Targets: Define clear and specific disarmament targets, such as reducing nuclear arsenals, limiting the production of small arms, and curbing the proliferation of conventional weapons. Goals should be measurable and time-bound to facilitate progress tracking.

- Comprehensive Scope: Address various categories of weapons, including nuclear, chemical, biological, and conventional arms. A holistic approach ensures that all aspects of disarmament are considered, reducing the overall threat of militarization.

2. Establishing Timelines:

- Short-Term Milestones: Create a timeline with short-term milestones—such as annual or biennial goals—that allow for incremental progress. These milestones can serve as benchmarks for accountability and motivate nations to stay on track.

- Long-Term Vision: Develop a long-term vision that outlines the ultimate objectives of global disarmament, including a commitment to achieving a world free of nuclear weapons or other categories of arms. This vision can guide policy and diplomatic efforts over the decades.

3. Accountability Measures:

- Regular Reporting: Require participating nations to submit regular reports detailing their progress toward disarmament goals. These reports should include data on arms stockpiles, production, and any measures taken to reduce military spending.

- Independent Verification: Establish independent verification mechanisms to assess compliance with disarmament commitments. Third-party organizations can conduct inspections and audits to ensure transparency and build trust among nations.

4. Incorporating Civilian Rights:

- Recognition of Responsible Ownership: Ensure that disarmament goals respect the rights of responsible civilian arms owners, including hunters, sport shooters, and collectors. Policies should differentiate between responsible ownership and illicit arms trade.

- Public Education Campaigns: Promote public education campaigns that inform citizens about responsible arms ownership and safety practices, helping to foster a culture of accountability among gun owners.

5. Combatting Corruption:

   - Anti-Corruption Provisions: Integrate anti-corruption measures into disarmament agreements, requiring nations to implement transparent practices in defense procurement and funding. This includes measures to combat bribery and ensure integrity in arms deals.

   - Monitoring Mechanisms: Establish mechanisms to monitor and report on corruption in the defense sector, allowing civil society organizations and independent watchdogs to play a role in ensuring accountability.

6. Building International Cooperation:

   - Global Partnerships: Encourage international cooperation and partnership among nations, NGOs, and civil society organizations to foster a collaborative approach to disarmament. These partnerships can enhance resources and expertise for achieving disarmament goals.

   - Regional Initiatives: Support regional disarmament initiatives that align with global goals, allowing nations to address specific security concerns while contributing to broader disarmament efforts.

7. Engaging Stakeholders:

- Inclusive Dialogue: Facilitate inclusive dialogue among governments, civil society, the private sector, and affected communities to ensure that disarmament goals reflect diverse perspectives and experiences. Engaging all stakeholders increases the legitimacy and effectiveness of disarmament initiatives.

- Youth and Education Programs: Involve youth in discussions about disarmament and global security, fostering a sense of responsibility and empowerment to advocate for peace in their communities.

8. Evaluation and Adaptation:

- Regular Review Processes: Establish regular review processes to assess the progress of disarmament goals and adjust strategies as needed. This adaptability will help respond to emerging challenges and shifting geopolitical landscapes.

- Feedback Mechanisms: Create feedback mechanisms that allow participants to share insights and lessons learned from disarmament efforts. Continuous improvement can enhance the effectiveness of initiatives over time.

By establishing clear global disarmament goals that include specific targets, timelines, and accountability measures, nations can work collaboratively toward a more peaceful and secure

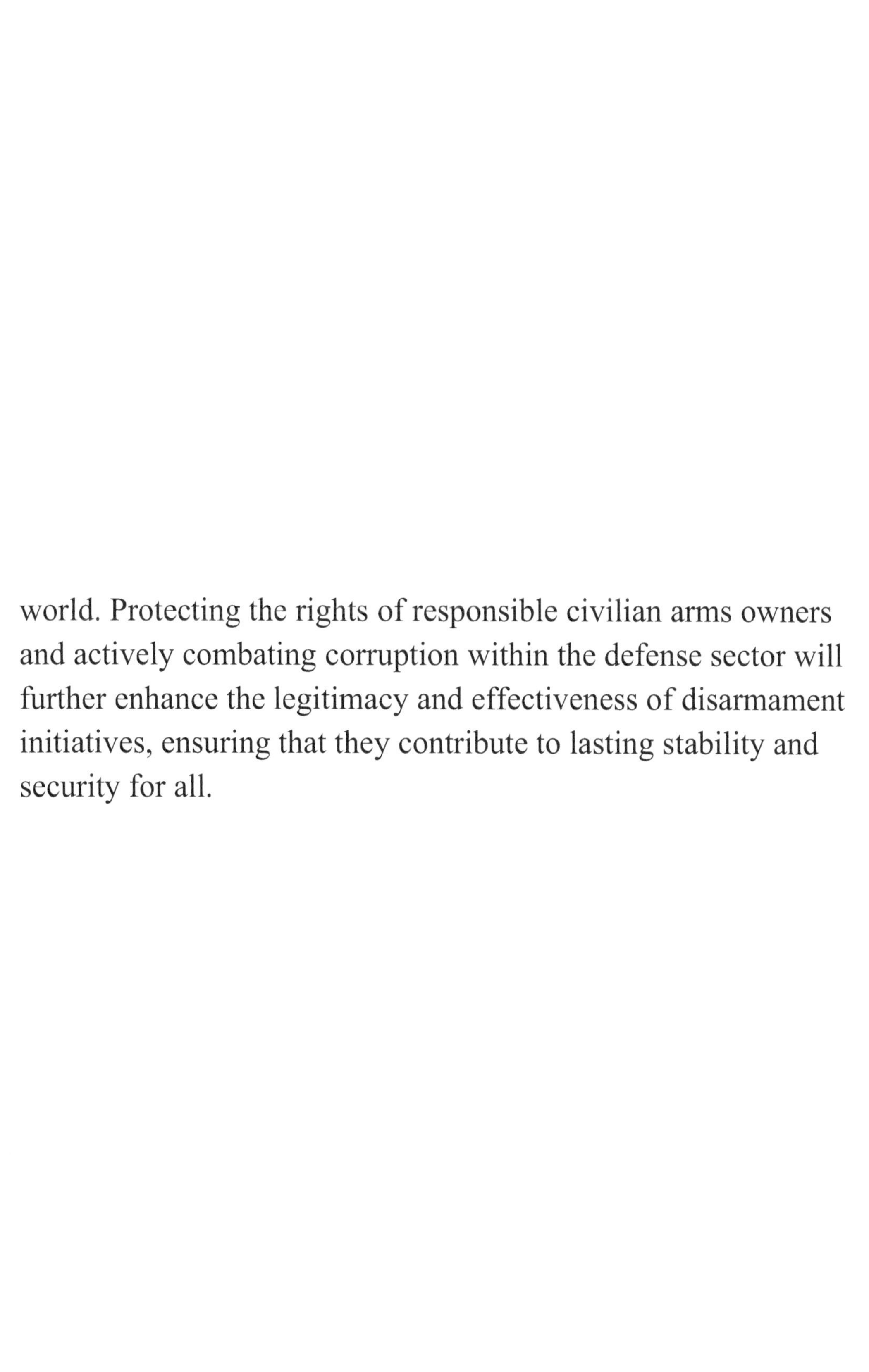

world. Protecting the rights of responsible civilian arms owners and actively combating corruption within the defense sector will further enhance the legitimacy and effectiveness of disarmament initiatives, ensuring that they contribute to lasting stability and security for all.

Aligning disarmament efforts with the United Nations Sustainable Development Goals (SDGs) is crucial for addressing the root causes of conflict while promoting peace and security. This alignment ensures that disarmament initiatives contribute not only to reducing weapons proliferation but also to fostering sustainable development, addressing poverty and inequality, and safeguarding the rights of responsible arms owners. Here are key components for implementing this approach:

1. Integrating Disarmament with SDGs:

 - Mapping Connections: Identify and articulate the connections between disarmament objectives and specific SDGs, such as Goal 16 (Peace, Justice, and Strong Institutions) and Goal 1 (No Poverty). Highlight how reducing militarization and arms proliferation can contribute to more stable and equitable societies.

 - Holistic Framework: Develop a holistic framework that incorporates disarmament as a key element of sustainable development strategies. This framework should emphasize the interdependence of peace, security, and development.

2. Addressing Root Causes of Conflict:

 - Poverty Reduction Initiatives: Implement development programs aimed at alleviating poverty and improving living standards in conflict-prone areas. Investing in education, healthcare, and economic opportunities can reduce grievances that lead to conflict.

 - Promoting Equality: Focus on initiatives that address inequality and social exclusion, ensuring that marginalized groups have access to resources and opportunities. Empowering vulnerable populations can enhance social cohesion and reduce the likelihood of violence.

3. Empowering Local Communities:

 - Community-Led Development: Encourage community-led development initiatives that prioritize local needs and solutions. Engaging communities in decision-making processes fosters ownership and accountability, promoting peace and security.

 - Youth and Education Programs: Invest in education programs that promote peacebuilding, conflict resolution, and responsible citizenship among young people. Educating youth about their rights and responsibilities can create a culture of non-violence and empowerment.

4. Safeguarding Rights to Responsible Arms Ownership:

- Regulatory Frameworks: Establish regulatory frameworks that recognize and protect the rights of responsible civilian arms owners while preventing misuse and illegal arms trafficking. Effective regulations can balance individual rights with public safety.

- Public Awareness Campaigns: Launch campaigns to educate citizens about responsible arms ownership practices, safety measures, and the ethical implications of arms use. Promoting responsible ownership can help mitigate risks associated with firearms.

5. Combatting Profit-Driven Motives:

- Transparency in Defense Spending: Promote transparency and accountability in defense spending and arms procurement processes. Encourage governments to allocate resources toward development and social programs rather than military expenditure driven by profit motives.

- Corporate Social Responsibility: Foster a culture of corporate social responsibility (CSR) within the defense industry, encouraging companies to prioritize ethical practices and community engagement over profit maximization. This can help align corporate interests with social good.

6. Strengthening Governance and Institutions:

   - Building Strong Institutions: Invest in strengthening governance and institutions that promote accountability, rule of law, and human rights. Effective governance can mitigate corruption and enhance the legitimacy of disarmament efforts.

   - Community Policing and Safety: Encourage community policing initiatives that foster trust between law enforcement and communities. Building positive relationships can enhance security and reduce reliance on militarization.

7. Monitoring and Evaluation:

   - Impact Assessments: Conduct regular impact assessments to evaluate the effectiveness of disarmament initiatives in achieving both disarmament goals and sustainable development outcomes. Use data to inform decision-making and improve program effectiveness.

   - Feedback Mechanisms: Establish feedback mechanisms that allow communities and stakeholders to share their experiences and insights regarding disarmament and development efforts. This input can enhance responsiveness and adaptability.

8. Global Partnerships:

   - Collaborative Approaches: Foster partnerships among governments, NGOs, and international organizations to align disarmament efforts with sustainable development initiatives.

Collaborative approaches can leverage resources and expertise for greater impact.

- Engaging Civil Society: Involve civil society organizations in the design and implementation of disarmament and development initiatives. Their insights and advocacy can enhance the relevance and effectiveness of programs.

By focusing on sustainable development and aligning disarmament efforts with the SDGs, nations can address the root causes of conflict, promote peace, and ensure that citizens retain their rights to responsible arms ownership. This comprehensive approach fosters a culture of accountability and collaboration, ultimately contributing to a more secure and equitable world.

Conclusion

Path to Global De-Escalation and Disarmament

The journey toward global de-escalation and disarmament is indeed a complex and challenging endeavor, yet it is essential for achieving lasting peace and security. To successfully navigate this path, a multifaceted strategy is required—one that integrates diplomacy, education, economic incentives, and cultural engagement. Below are key components of this strategy that can foster cooperation and understanding among nations while ensuring the protection of individual rights and addressing the pervasive issues of corruption and the influence of the military-industrial complex.

1. Diplomatic Initiatives:

 - Multi-Track Diplomacy: Engage in multi-track diplomacy that includes formal government negotiations, informal dialogues, and participation from civil society, NGOs, and grassroots movements. This inclusive approach can facilitate broader understanding and consensus on disarmament goals.

 - Bilateral and Multilateral Agreements: Promote bilateral and multilateral treaties focused on arms reduction, transparency, and verification measures. Such agreements can create a framework for accountability and mutual trust among nations.

2. Educational Programs:

 - Awareness and Advocacy: Implement educational campaigns to raise awareness about the implications of militarization, the importance of responsible arms ownership, and the need for disarmament. Engaging communities in these discussions can empower them to advocate for peace.

 - Conflict Resolution Training: Provide training in conflict resolution and negotiation skills to community leaders, youth, and educators. Equipping individuals with these skills can foster peaceful dialogue and reduce the likelihood of conflicts escalating into violence.

3. Economic Incentives:

 - Development Aid and Investment: Allocate development aid and investment to countries that commit to disarmament. Encourage governments to redirect military spending toward social programs, infrastructure, and education that benefit citizens.

 - Incentivizing Compliance: Establish economic incentives for nations that demonstrate progress in disarmament efforts, such as debt relief, trade benefits, or access to development grants. These incentives can motivate countries to prioritize peace over militarization.

4. Cultural Engagement:

 - Cultural Exchange Programs: Promote cultural exchange initiatives that foster understanding and cooperation among diverse populations. By building relationships through art, music, and dialogue, communities can develop a shared commitment to peace.

 - Storytelling and Narratives: Encourage storytelling initiatives that highlight diverse human experiences related to conflict and peace. These narratives can create empathy and understanding, breaking down stereotypes and fostering solidarity.

5. Combating Corruption:

- Transparency and Accountability: Advocate for transparency in defense spending and arms procurement. Establishing independent oversight mechanisms can help combat corruption and ensure that military resources are used ethically.

- Community Involvement: Engage local communities in monitoring defense expenditures and advocating for responsible governance. Empowering citizens to hold their leaders accountable can reduce the influence of corrupt practices in the military sector.

6. Protecting Individual Rights:

- Regulatory Frameworks for Arms Ownership: Develop regulatory frameworks that respect the rights of responsible civilian arms owners while preventing misuse and illegal arms trade. These frameworks should prioritize public safety without infringing on individual rights.

- Public Education on Responsible Ownership: Conduct educational programs on responsible arms ownership, emphasizing safety, ethics, and the importance of community engagement in discussions about firearms.

7. Fostering Cooperation and Understanding:

- Collaborative Research Initiatives: Support collaborative research projects that examine the social, economic, and political impacts of militarization and disarmament. Sharing knowledge and expertise can inform effective policy decisions.

  - Engaging International Organizations: Collaborate with international organizations and regional bodies to enhance global efforts toward disarmament and peace. These partnerships can amplify advocacy and provide platforms for dialogue.

8. Long-Term Commitment:

  - Sustained Engagement: Recognize that achieving global de-escalation and disarmament is a long-term commitment that requires ongoing engagement, adaptation, and resilience. Continuous dialogue and collaboration are essential to address evolving security threats.

  - Evaluation and Reflection: Establish mechanisms for evaluating the impact of disarmament initiatives and learning from successes and challenges. Reflecting on experiences can inform future strategies and enhance effectiveness.

By implementing a multifaceted strategy that combines diplomacy, education, economic incentives, and cultural engagement, we can create a conducive environment for global de-escalation and disarmament. Fostering cooperation and understanding among nations, respecting individual rights, and combating corruption will pave the way for a safer, more peaceful world where governments prioritize the well-being of their citizens and communities over military profit and influence. Achieving this vision requires collective action, commitment, and a shared belief in the possibilities of peace and cooperation.

When global governments shift their financial priorities from weapons and military spending to philanthropic governance and development initiatives, several significant outcomes can be anticipated. This transition could have profound implications for social stability, economic development, and international relations. Here are some potential effects:

1. Enhanced Social Welfare

- Improved Public Services: Redirecting funds from military expenditures to social programs can lead to better healthcare, education, infrastructure, and social services. This investment in human capital can improve quality of life and public well-being.

- Reduction in Poverty and Inequality: Increased funding for development initiatives can help address poverty and reduce inequality. Programs focused on job creation, skill development, and economic opportunities can empower marginalized communities and foster social cohesion.

- Decreased Militarization: A reduction in military spending can lead to decreased militarization of societies. Governments may focus more on diplomatic solutions to conflicts and invest in peacebuilding initiatives rather than military interventions.

- Lower Risk of Conflict: By addressing root causes of conflict, such as poverty, inequality, and lack of opportunity, governments can reduce the likelihood of civil unrest and international conflicts. Investing in education and social programs can promote stability.

- Increased Diplomatic Engagement: A focus on philanthropic governance can enhance diplomatic relations among countries. Collaborative projects that address global challenges, such as climate change, health crises, and economic disparities, can foster goodwill and mutual understanding.

- Strengthened Multilateral Institutions: Governments may become more supportive of international organizations and agreements aimed at promoting peace, development, and cooperation, leading to a more unified global approach to addressing pressing issues.

4. Economic Transformation

- Diversification of Economies: Transitioning financial resources from military industries to development can foster innovation and diversification in economies. This shift can create new industries and job opportunities in sectors like renewable energy, technology, and sustainable agriculture.

- Long-Term Economic Growth: Investments in education, healthcare, and infrastructure can lead to long-term economic growth by creating a healthier, more educated workforce capable of contributing to the economy.

5. Enhanced Governance and Accountability

- Focus on Good Governance: Philanthropic governance emphasizes transparency, accountability, and citizen engagement. Governments may prioritize good governance practices, leading to more effective and responsive institutions.

- Empowerment of Civil Society: Increased funding for community-based initiatives and NGOs can empower civil society organizations, enabling them to play a crucial role in governance and development processes.

6. Shift in Military Industry Dynamics

- Reduction in Defense Industry Influence: A decrease in military spending may lessen the influence of the defense industry on government policies. This could lead to more balanced discussions about national priorities and security strategies.

- Reallocation of Defense Resources: Defense contractors may need to adapt to a changing market by diversifying their portfolios and investing in non-military technologies and services.

7. Challenges and Considerations

- Resistance from Established Interests: Transitioning away from military spending may face resistance from entrenched political and economic interests tied to the defense industry. Advocacy and coalition-building will be essential to overcome these challenges.

- Balancing Security Needs: While focusing on philanthropic governance, governments must still address legitimate security concerns to maintain national and international stability. A careful balance between development and security priorities will be necessary.

Moving finances from weapons to philanthropic governance has the potential to create a more peaceful, equitable, and prosperous world. This shift can lead to enhanced social welfare, reduced conflict, stronger international cooperation, and economic transformation. However, it requires a commitment from governments, civil society, and international organizations to pursue this vision collaboratively while addressing the challenges that arise during this transition. Ultimately, prioritizing human development over militarization can contribute to a more sustainable and harmonious global society.